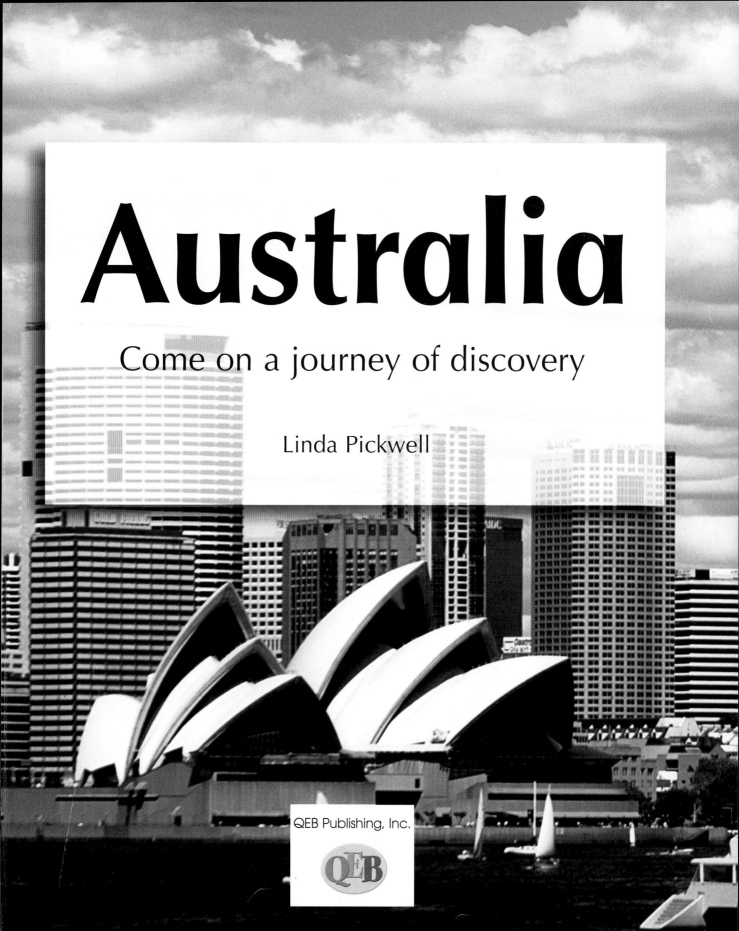

Australia

Come on a journey of discovery

Linda Pickwell

QEB Publishing, Inc.

QEB

Published in the United States by
QEB Publishing
23062 La Cadena Drive
Laguna Hills
Irvine
CA 92653

Library of Congress Control Number 2004101780

ISBN 1-59566-058-5

Written by Elaine Jackson
Designed by Starry Dog Books Ltd
Editor Christine Harvey
Map by PCGraphics (UK) Ltd

Creative Director Louise Morley
Editorial Manager Jean Coppendale

Picture credits

Key: t = top, b = bottom, m = middle, c = center,
l = left, r = right

Ecoscene /Kjell Sandved 5tr, /Papilio/R Pickett 6,
/Neeraj Mishra 30tl, /Karl Ammann 11t, 30tr, /Sally
Morgan 15, 30br, /Luc Hosten 22, /Kjell Sandved 23tr,
/Papilio/Robert Gill 26, /Luc Hosten 28bl, /Stephen
Coyne 29.
Getty Images Front Cover, Michael Wong, /Jack
Hollingsworth 4–5, 30bl, /Johnny Johnson 7, /K Begg
8–9, /9cr, /Art Wolfe 11b, /Stan Osolinski 12–13,
/Johan Elzenga 14, /Pascal Crapet 16, /Johan
Elzenga 17, /Harald Sund 1, 18–19, /Daryl Balfour 20,
/Renee Lynn 21, /Tim Davis 23bl, /Gavriel Jecan
24bl, /Art Wolfe 24–25, /Douglas-Hamilton 28tr.
Ardea/D.Parer & E. Parer-Cook 10
Corbis Bob Walden 7br,10,/Keven Fleming 11br/
Paul A. Souders 12,/Photowood inc 17 t,/
Charles O' Rear 22tl,/John Van Hasselt 25br,/
Robert Essel 27tr.
Additional photography Jean Coppendale,
front cover, 3

Printed and bound in China

The words in **bold**
are explained in the
Glossary on page 28.

Contents

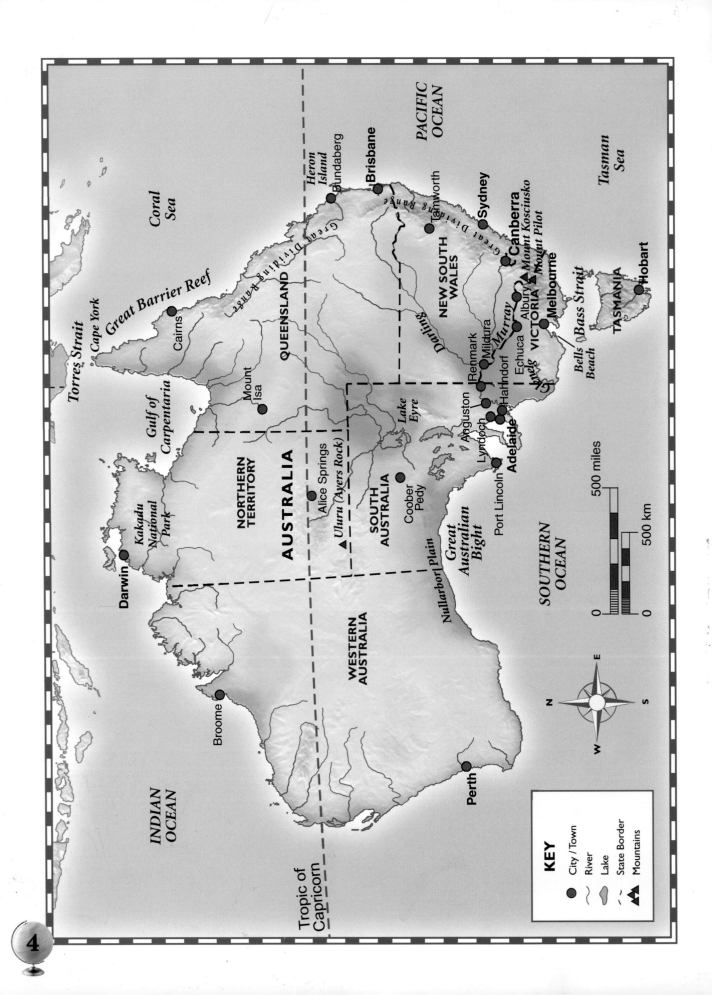

PACIFIC OCEAN

Tasman Sea

Coral Sea

Heron Island
Bundaberg
Brisbane

Tamworth
Sydney
Canberra
Mount Kosciusko
Mount Pilot
Melbourne
Hobart

Great Dividing Range

NEW SOUTH WALES

Great Barrier Reef

Cape York

Torres Strait

Cairns

QUEENSLAND

Darling

Murray

Albury
VICTORIA
Echuca
Renmark
Mildura
Hahndorf

TASMANIA

Bass Strait

Bells Beach

Gulf of Carpentaria

Mount Isa

Lake Eyre

Anguston
Lyndoch
Adelaide

Alice Springs

NORTHERN TERRITORY

AUSTRALIA

Uluru (Ayers Rock)

SOUTH AUSTRALIA

Coober Pedy

Port Lincoln

Great Australian Bight

SOUTHERN OCEAN

500 miles

500 km

Kakadu National Park

Darwin

WESTERN AUSTRALIA

Nullarbor Plain

N
E
W
S

Broome

INDIAN OCEAN

Perth

Tropic of Capricorn

KEY

- City / Town
- River
- Lake
- State Border
- Mountains

4

Where in the world is Australia?

Australia lies south of the Asian **continent**. It is the smallest continent in the world, but one of the largest countries. There are about 18 million people in the country, most of them in towns and cities near the coast.

Did you know?

The island of Tasmania is part of Australia. It lies 190 miles off the south-eastern coast, near Melbourne. Long ago, it was linked to the mainland of Australia, but was separated after the last Ice Age when the Bass Strait was formed by rising water levels.

▼ Australia and its place in the world

Australia

▲ Australia's flag

Did you know?

Name
Commonwealth of Australia
Location
South of the continent of Asia
Nearest neighbors
Papua New Guinea, Indonesia and Malaysia to the north, New Zealand to the south-east
Surrounding oceans
Pacific Ocean, Indian Ocean
Length of coastline 16,100 miles
Capital Canberra in New South Wales
Area 2,967,909 square miles
Population 18,000,000
Life expectancy Male: 75, Female: 80
Religion Christianity
Languages Australian English and many Aboriginal languages
Climate Generally arid, temperate in the south and east, **tropical** in the north
Highest mountain range Mount Kosciusko (7,316 feet)
Major rivers Murray (length: 1,609 miles), Darling (length:1,700 miles)
Currency Australian dollar

What is Australia like?

The regions
Different areas of Australia were developed and named as explorers from around the world arrived in the country. There are six regions on mainland Australia: New South Wales, Victoria, Queensland, South Australia, Western Australia, and the Northern Territory.

The outback
Australia is the driest and flattest of the **continents**. Two-thirds of the country is desert or semidesert.

▼ Kimberley in north-west Australia is one of the world's last great areas of wilderness.

The vast desert areas are referred to as the "outback." These areas have little habitation and poor vegetation, mainly due to lack of rain. The semidesert parts have sheep and cattle farms on them called "stations." Ninety percent of the population live in the cities and towns around the coast.

Western Australia
The vast **plateau** in the inland part of western Australia is rich in ancient rocks and minerals. Since the area was first discovered, miners have endured harsh conditions in the hope of striking gold. Australia is the world's largest producer of industrial diamonds and opals.

The Great Dividing Range

This is a series of mountain ranges that stretch from Cape York at the most northern tip of Queensland to the Bass Strait in the south. These mountain ranges contain the Blue Mountains and the Australian Alps.

The Central Basin

This is a flat area stretching from the Gulf of Carpentaria in the north, to the mouth of the Murray River in the south. Thousands of years ago this was an inland sea.

▲ "The Three Sisters" rock formations are at Katoomba in the Blue Mountains near Sydney. At night they are floodlit.

Australia has a number of national parks. Jon visited the National Park of Kakadu and wrote to his English penpal about it.

I visited the Kakadu National Park yesterday, where the movie "Crocodile Dundee" was filmed. I saw the cave paintings done by the Aboriginal people, and went on a dawn cruise along the Yellow Water to see the birds and crocodiles. It was awesome!

◄ Australian crocodiles can run very fast on land and can leap up out of the water to catch and drown their prey.

Climate

Around the country

Australia has a **tropical** or near-tropical climate. Two-thirds of the land is desert or shrubland, and has little rainfall. These areas can be hot during the day, but cold at night. The **interior** has little rainfall and long droughts occur. Rainfall is important, because it is needed to sustain all plant and animal life.

The seasons

The summer months, December to February, are hot throughout the country. If you traveled here on Christmas Day you might spend it with other Australians on the beach! The winter months, June to August, are usually the coolest and wettest.

The north

People say that there are only two seasons in the north—the dry and the wet. During the summer months, the sun is above northern Australia. This brings high temperatures to the area. It also brings **monsoon** rains.

The south

The southern areas have warm summers and mild winters.

The east

Winds blowing from the Pacific Ocean and rising over the Great Dividing Range can bring heavy rains in late spring, summer, and early fall.

▼ *The arid regions have little vegetation.*

Maximum temperatures

City	January	April	July	October
Darwin	90°F	91°F	88°F	93°F
Perth	84°F	75°F	63°F	70°F
Melbourne	79°F	68°F	55°F	66°F
Brisbane	84°F	79°F	68°F	81°F

Average monthly rainfall

City	January	April	July	October
Darwin	15 in	3⅘ in	0 in	2 in
Perth	⅓ in	1⅔ in	6½ in	2¼ in
Melbourne	1⅘ in	2¼ in	1⅘ in	2½ in
Brisbane	6⅖ in	3¾ in	2¼ in	2½ in

▼ Surfer's Paradise south of Brisbane is a very popular beach. In the hot sun, people are advised to protect their skin and wear a t-shirt and a hat.

Australia's wildlife

Unique plants and animals

Australia has developed a unique range of plants and animals that have **adapted** to the low rainfall and poor soil. Australia has more than 25,000 species of plants and around 250,000 species of animal life.

The tropical rainforests in the east are some of the oldest **ecosystems** in the world. The tree kangaroo and the birdwing butterfly live in this habitat.

The Australian bush

Near the coast, in the east, south-east, and south-west, are open woodlands. These areas are generally referred to as the Australian bush.

Eucalyptus trees grow here and can withstand drought, bush fires, and poor soil. Gray kangaroos and koalas live only in these areas.

Australia is famous for marsupials. These are extinct everywhere else in the world, except for South America. The best known are the kangaroo and the smaller wallaby. Birds, such as kookaburras, parrots, and budgerigars, are also found in the bush.

Dangerous creatures

Australia is the home of more deadly spiders and reptiles than anywhere else in the world. The deadliest spider is the redback and the worst snake is the taipan. The most dangerous animal to humans is the saltwater crocodile of northern Australia.

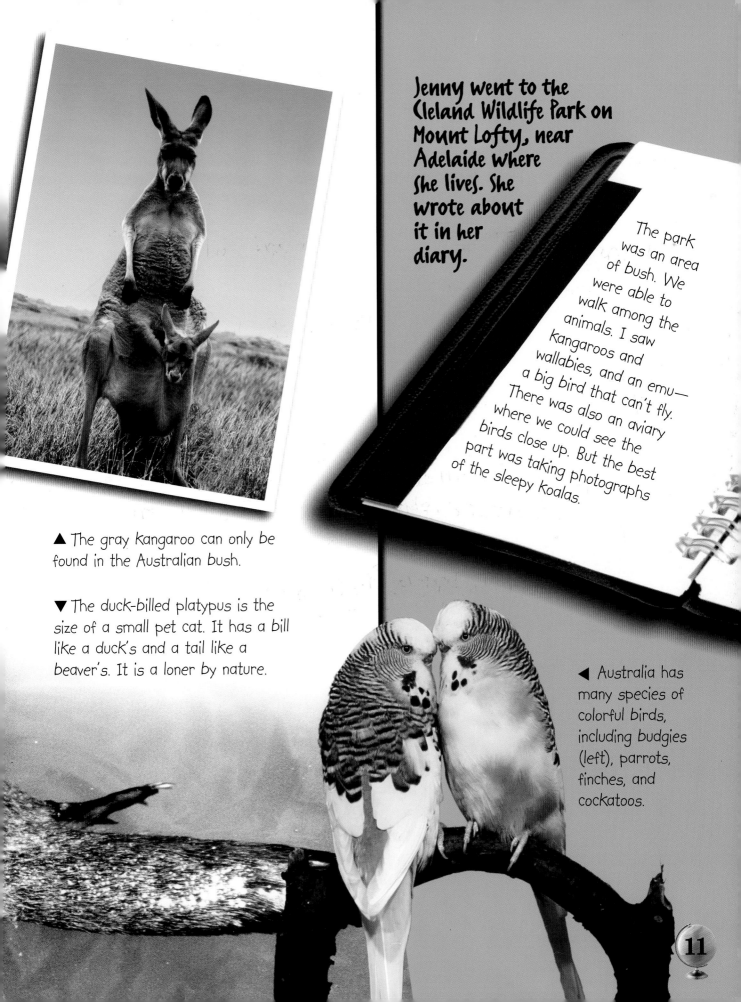

Jenny went to the Cleland Wildlife Park on Mount Lofty, near Adelaide where she lives. She wrote about it in her diary.

The park was an area of bush. We were able to walk among the animals. I saw kangaroos and wallabies, and an emu—a big bird that can't fly. There was also an aviary where we could see the birds close up. But the best part was taking photographs of the sleepy koalas.

▲ The gray kangaroo can only be found in the Australian bush.

▼ The duck-billed platypus is the size of a small pet cat. It has a bill like a duck's and a tail like a beaver's. It is a loner by nature.

◄ Australia has many species of colorful birds, including budgies (left), parrots, finches, and cockatoos.

Traveling around Australia

By air

Australia has a number of international airports, in Sydney, Melbourne, Perth, Brisbane, Cairns, Adelaide, Darwin, and Hobart in Tasmania. In 1934, the airline QANTAS began some of the first international flights in the world.

If you want to travel within the country, there are a number of smaller airports you can use. Traveling by air allows the vast distances of the country to be covered more quickly.

▶ John Flynn started the Flying Doctor service in 1928.

The Flying Doctor

For many people living in the **interior,** the nearest hospital may be several hours away by car. To help solve this problem, the Flying Doctor service was started. Doctors use small, lightweight planes to reach remote **settlements** or homesteads.

▼ In 1885 Melbourne's first tram made the journey from the city to the suburbs.

By train

Australia doesn't have a railway network that reaches all areas of the country. Most main lines are around the coast. There is one major line across the center of the country, from the main cities in the south to Darwin.

Journey	Distance	Flying time
Sydney to Perth	2,215 miles	5 hours
Adelaide to Darwin	1,625 miles	3½ hours

Many people make special train journeys to see the country, and the trains offering this service are like moving hotels. One of them is the Indian Pacific Route. This takes three days from Sydney to Perth. The train crosses the Nullarbor **Plain**, a vast part of the Great Victoria Desert in Western Australia, on the world's longest length of straight track.

By road

Today, there is a national highway network, linking all the capital cities of the regions. Most goods are transported by road. Road transporters can be three to five "trucks" long. Most Australians own a car and use the highway systems. In cities there is a mix of car, bus, and tram travel, and Sydney has an overhead monorail.

Traveling through the cities

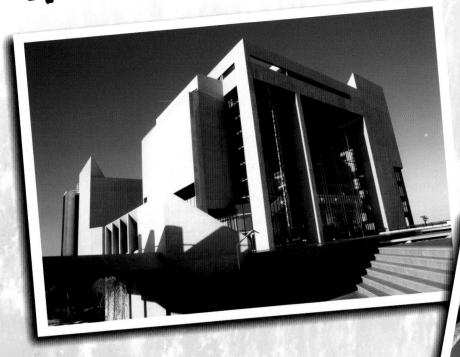

◀ Canberra is the home of Australia's High Court and the National University. It is also the financial heart of Australia, and the center of government.

▼ Adelaide hosts many popular arts festivals.

Canberra

This is the capital city of Australia in the state of New South Wales. It was originally a small sheep station by the Molonglo River. Traveling here today you will see that it is the country's political center. It is a modern city with stores and restaurants, as well as areas of national parklands.

Adelaide

In 1836, the flat **plain** between the Mount Lofty Ranges was chosen as the place to build the city of Adelaide, the capital of South Australia. Traveling here you will see many 19th-century public buildings, including the state library, museum, and art gallery. Although proud of its past, the city is very modern, with many stores and theaters.

▲ There's plenty to do in Perth, including surfing, yacht racing and humpback whale-watching.

Perth
On the west coast, Perth is Australia's most isolated state capital. It lies on the Swan River, 6 miles from the Indian Ocean. From the first settlers' houses, the city has grown as the gold rush and mining brought wealth to the area. On one side of the city there are beaches, and inland, many parks.

Melbourne
Melbourne, on the south coast, is a relaxed city that offers many outdoor activities. The city is a mix of impressive skyscrapers and 19th-century buildings; you can even travel around by old-fashioned tram. Nearby are areas of great natural beauty, such as Philip Island, the Yarra Valley, and the Dandenong mountain foothills.

Brisbane
On the east coast, Brisbane is surrounded by green and hilly suburbs. The town center is a mix of modern buildings made of glass and steel, and 19th century buildings. Within the city is a bustling area with an Asian community, known as Chinatown.

A tour of Sydney

Emma and Andrew are twins. They live in Sydney in New South Wales. Their American cousins are coming to visit and the twins have made them a city guide.

Circular Quay

Sydney is a big city and can be split into four areas. Our favorite is Circular Quay. It is the oldest part, dating back to 1788 when the first ships arrived from Britain. We sometimes go to the Sydney Opera House, which has a variety of theaters and concert halls. It is on Bennelong Point, which sticks out into the harbor.

Royal Botanic Gardens

We like the quiet part of the city best. There is a large parkland, called the Royal Botanic Gardens. It was established in 1816 and has two glasshouses that hold mini **tropical ecosystems**. We will take you to the Governor's private garden, which is now open to the public. Open-air concerts are held here. We can take a picnic!

Did you know?

Sydney Opera House facts:

It holds 3,000 events per year.

It has an annual audience of 2 million people.

It has more than a million roof tiles.

Darling Harbor

We'll also take you to Darling Harbor. There's so much to do there. You can visit the huge aquarium and walk along a clear tunnel with colorful fish swimming all round you. It feels as if you're walking on the sea floor! There's also the biggest movie screen I've ever seen, and a real Chinese garden with huge fish in the pond.

Sydney Harbor Bridge

Another famous sight is the Sydney Harbor Bridge, completed in 1932. It is a single-span bridge and took eight years to build. Sydney is an important business and shopping center. It is always busy during the day with workers and shoppers, and at night with people going to restaurants, cafés, and theaters.

The Great Barrier Reef

History of the Great Barrier Reef

This is a natural wonder found off the Queensland coast. It is the largest **coral** reef in the world. Coral can be dated back at least 500 million years.

The Great Barrier Reef began about 18,000 years ago during the last Ice Age. It is a major tourist attraction and is protected by the Marine Park Authority, established by an act of Parliament in 1975. People from all over the world travel to the area to experience diving, snorkeling, or to look at the colorful coral reef from glass-bottomed boats.

More than 2,000 species of fish and countless numbers of corals, both hard and soft, are found in these waters.

▼ *The coral reef is a fragile ecosystem.*

▼ *Shoals of reef fish are every color of the rainbow.*

Scott went to stay with his friend Tom. Tom's dad took them to the Great Barrier Reef. Scott wrote to his family about some of the amazing sights he saw.

I wish you could be here. We had a trip in a glass-bottomed boat. We could look down at the fish and coral—it was amazing! We saw a great shoal of bat fish, which live in colonies. There were lots of colorful, small fish and a moray eel, which must have been 6½ feet long. But even better were the two times we went snorkeling. Being in the water and so close to the wildlife is fantastic. Yesterday, potato cod were swimming next to us and a manta ray came close enough to touch.

Mom, Dad & Chloe
34 Wongaboo Rise
Mellhill
Vangswith
2905WA

▼ Divers should take care not to touch the coral or it will be damaged.

Traveling along the Murray River

The source of the river

The Murray River is the largest river in Australia and a vital source of water. The **source** of the river is near Mount Kosciusko in the Snowy Mountains, part of the eastern mountain ranges. The river has been known to dry up on at least three occasions. The river flows through the city of Adelaide and into the Great Australian Bight.

The upper river

Cutting through the eastern mountains, the upper river flows west and north-west, forming most of the New South Wales and Victoria **state** boundaries. The central section lies on a floodplain with a number of **tributaries** joining it.

▼ A paddlesteamer on the Murray River.

EMMYLOU

Monitoring the water

The importance of the Murray River for drinking water and **irrigation** led to the formation of the River Valley Commission in 1915. It is responsible for developing **hydroelectric power** and monitoring the quality and use of the water.

The history of the river

Paddlesteamers were important in developing **settlements** along the Murray River. They were used to carry goods between areas. An ex-convict, Henry Hopwood, began a ferry-crossing service at Echuca in 1835.

Echuca eventually became the largest inland port in Australia.

Today, the town has developed this history of the river into a tourist attraction. There are horse-drawn carriages on the streets and paddlesteamers on the river, so people can see what the river and the areas around it used to be like.

Drew is doing a project on the history of the Murray River at school.

Water from the Murray River was first used for irrigation in 1887 when the Canadian brothers William and George Chaffey came to the town of Mildura. They established an irrigation system there. Mildura has now grown into a modern city surrounded by a region growing vines, olives, and citrus fruit.

The Barossa Valley

The Barossa Valley is the major wine-producing area of South Australia. It lies 30 miles north-east of the city of Adelaide in the Mount Lofty Ranges.

The history of the Barossa Valley

The area was first settled in 1842 by German immigrants who established the villages of Tanunda, Lyndoch, and Light's Pass. The climate helped them farm the land. The winter rains and warm summers encouraged good crops to grow in the soil. Grapes soon became the major crop and many wineries developed.

▲ At many Australian wineries you can watch the wine being made.

Tourist attractions

Traveling to this area, it is easy to see that the early German influence is still obvious in the style of the buildings and place names, and the region's food, music, and festivals.

Some of the largest wineries are now open to the public as tourist attractions. The Collingrove Homestead at Anguston is now owned by the National Trust. It was built in 1856 and has been preserved to show the original furnishings.

▼ A view of the vines being grown in the Barossa Valley.

▲ This Lutheran church is in Hahndorf, named after Dirk Hahn, the captain of the first settlers' ship.

As a birthday treat, Anna asked for a trip to Hahndorf. She wrote about her day there in her diary.

My great-great-grandfather lived in Germany as a small child before he moved to South Australia. The first settlers arrived from Germany in Hahndorf in 1838 on a ship called the 'Zebra'. I liked looking at the German-style houses. There were many things on sale in the stores, from special German food to gifts and candy. I had a ride through the town on a horse-drawn carriage. I enjoyed the atmosphere and tried to imagine what life would have been like for the settlers.

Alice Springs and Uluru

Alice Springs

The main **settlement** in the "Red Center," a large area of desert and rocky ridges in the Northern Territory, is called Alice Springs. It became a staging post in 1871 for the overland telegraph line and is named after Alice Todd, the wife of the line's construction manager.

There was no fully surfaced road until the 1940s. Today, the railway and the cross-continental **Stuart Highway** make it an important transport town for beef and minerals.

Tourist attraction

Alice Springs is a major tourist attraction with an average of 400,000 visitors every year. Traveling there, you will see the Museum of Central Australia, original settlement buildings, and the only winery in central Australia, Chateau Hornsby.

Uluru

Many visitors to Alice Springs visit the Uluru-Kata Tjuta National Park, which contains the famous landmark of Uluru (this is the Aboriginal name for Ayers Rock). This giant rock is made of a type of sandstone called arkosic, which appears to change color according to the light. It is often photographed at sunset when it looks a fiery red-orange color.

Uluru is oval shaped, 12,672 feet in length and 6,600 feet wide. Shallow caves that are sacred to the **Aborigines** lie at the base of the rock. They contain carvings and paintings. Some of the more sacred sites are fenced off.

The Aborigines

Uluru is an important place in the culture of the Anangu Aborigines. In 1985, ownership of this site was formally handed back to them.

▼ Uluru stands 1,100 feet above the surrounding flat desert.

▲ In 2004 Darwin was added to the Ghan train's route from Adelaide.

▶ This Aboriginal rock art of handprints may be 4,000 years old.

The Aborigines

The history of the Aborigines

The **Aborigines** are the original inhabitants of Australia, and can be traced back 40,000 years. When Europeans came to claim Australia, many Aborigines were killed in fights over land. During the 1850s, Aborigines were placed in **reserves.**

Aboriginal people now form 1.6 percent of the population in Australia. Only recently has there been a real acceptance of their rights and some land given back to them.

Boomerangs

Traditionally, Aborigines lived as nomadic hunters. They used special sticks called boomerangs. The boomerang was used in a variety of ways—as a weapon, in traditional

games, and even for poking a fire! Over time the shape has changed and now the stick curves and returns to the thrower when hurled. Many boomerangs are decorated with pictures telling stories and myths.

Dreamtime
The Aborigines base much of their culture on "Dreamtime." These are special stories based in myths about the creation of the world. The Aborigines believe that giant beings called "creation ancestors" created the world with their movements.

Aborigine children
Most Aborigine children attend public schools, called state schools. The Australian government now insists on equal opportunities for all and have included Aboriginal culture in the education curriculum.

▲ Young Aborigine children surf the Internet for study and for fun.

▲ Boomerang means "throwing stick".

Namatjira goes to a small school in the outback. This is an extract from his diary.

◄ Aboriginal art, painted on bark or canvas, is in great demand from art galleries, especially Australian ones.

Today we performed a special dance for some visitors to our school. It was a sequence about a serpent creating flat lands with its sideways movements. We told them what Dreamtime is and how we had represented the movements and moods of nature in our dance. I hope they enjoyed it.

27

Glossary

Aborigine
the original people to inhabit Australia

adapted
Changed to suit the environment

coral
hard material that forms from the skeletons of tiny sea animals

continent
one of the seven large areas of land on the Earth's surface: Africa, Asia, Australasia, Antarctica, North America, South America, and Europe

ecosystem
living creatures and their environment, and how they affect each other

hydroelectric power
electricity made from the controlled flow of water

interior
central land not near the coast

irrigation
supplying water to the land, usually to support agriculture

marsupials
mammals that carry their young in a pouch

monsoon
the rainy season—heavy downpours often experienced in hot countries

plain
an extensive area of level land, usually at a low altitude

plateau
an extensive area of mainly level land at a high altitude

reserve
public land set aside for housing certain groups of people

settlement
a place where people set up a community

source
where a river or stream starts

Stuart Highway
a major highway, named after the explorer John McDougall Stuart, which crosses the country and passes through Alice Springs

tributaries
river or stream that runs into another, often larger, one

tropical
a climate that is hot, wet and humid

Index

Teaching ideas and activities for children

The **Travel Through** series offers up-to-date information and interdisciplinary knowledge in subject areas such as geography, language arts, numeracy, history, and social studies. The series enables children to develop an overview ("the big picture") of each country.

This overview reflects the huge diversity and richness of the life and culture of each country. The series aims to prevent the development of misconceptions, stereotypes, and prejudices, which often develop when the focus of a study narrows too quickly onto a small locality within a country. The books will help children gain access to this overview, and also develop an understanding of the interconnectedness of places. They contribute to children's geographical knowledge, skills, and understanding, and help them to make sense of the world around them.

The following activities promote thinking skills and creativity. The activities in section A are designed to help children develop critical thinking skills, while the activities in section B are designed to promote different types of learning styles.

A: ACTIVITIES TO DEVELOP THINKING SKILLS
ACTIVITIES TO PROMOTE RESEARCH AND RECALL OF FACTS
Ask the children to:
• write a list of all the facts they know about Australia. Visit these lists later to check accuracy.
• investigate living in the interior of Australia—how to cope with the heat, water conservation, growing tourism, and distances to travel.

ACTIVITIES TO PROMOTE UNDERSTANDING
Ask the children to:
• describe climate changes between the coastal areas in the north, east, south, and west.

describe how life differs living on a sheep station in the outback from living in a coastal city.

ACTIVITIES TO PROMOTE THE USE OF KNOWLEDGE AND SKILLS TO SOLVE PROBLEMS

Ask the children to:

• decide how to cross a river containing saltwater crocodiles safely.
• draw a sequence of pictures to illustrate and explain the formation of coral.

ACTIVITIES TO ENCOURAGE ANALYTICAL THINKING

Ask the children to:

• discuss the best way to travel across the country, to the interior or within a city.
• write a poem describing the size of Australia, trying to give the feeling of space in the inlands and bustle of the cities.

ACTIVITIES TO PROMOTE CREATIVITY

Ask the children to:

• use collage or weaving to depict the colors of the areas of Australia—the coastal regions, the rainforest, and the arid interior.
• compose a mimed Aboriginal dream sequence.

ACTIVITIES TO HELP CHILDREN USE EVIDENCE TO FORM OPINIONS AND EVALUATE CONSEQUENCES OF DECISIONS

Ask the children to:

• discuss what value and what concerns tourism brings to the Great Barrier Reef or Uluru.
• discuss the rights and traditions of the Aborigines.

B: ACTIVITIES BASED ON DIFFERENT LEARNING STYLES

ACTIVITIES FOR LINGUISTIC LEARNERS

Ask the children to:

• write a list of instructions for someone wanting to backpack across Australia.
• write a poem to illustrate the size and complexity of the country.

ACTIVITIES FOR LOGICAL AND MATHEMATICAL LEARNERS

Ask the children to:

• examine the time differences between Australia and other countries.
• identify a region and list the main features.

ACTIVITIES FOR VISUAL LEARNERS

Ask the children to:
• locate stated cities or features on a map of Australia.
• design a poster or leaflet to encourage visitors either to the country or to a particular region.
• design a menu for a barbeque.

ACTIVITIES FOR KINESTHETIC LEARNERS

Ask the children to:
• use materials to create a representation of a famous landmark in Australia.

ACTIVITIES FOR MUSICAL LEARNERS

Ask the children to:
• compose a song, tune, or rap to celebrate the coming of rain in one of the dry areas.
• learn to sing an Australian folk song.

ACTIVITIES FOR INTER-PERSONAL LEARNERS

Ask the children to:
• work in a group to develop a presentation on one aspect of Australian life.
• work as a group to develop a sketch or short play about settling in Australia as pioneers.

ACTIVITIES FOR INTRA-PERSONAL LEARNERS

Ask the children to:
• describe how they would feel if they were lost in the outback.
• look at photographs of different regions and describe the environment.

ACTIVITIES FOR NATURALISTIC LEARNERS

Ask the children to:
• prepare an argument, either for increasing tourism or limiting tourism.